Boost eBay Sales!

How Great Entrepreneurs Can Boost Their EBAY Sales By 200% Using These Tips and Tricks

Tomas Snarskis
2018

© Copyright 2018 by Tomas Snarskis - All rights reserved.

This document is geared towards providing exact and reliable information in regards to the topic and issue covered. The publication is sold with the idea that the publisher is not required to render accounting, officially permitted, or otherwise, qualified services. If advice is necessary, legal or professional, a practiced individual in the profession should be ordered.

- From a Declaration of Principles which was accepted and approved equally by a Committee of the American Bar Association and a Committee of Publishers and Associations.

In no way is it legal to reproduce, duplicate, or transmit any part of this document in either electronic means or in printed format. Recording of this publication is strictly prohibited and any storage of this document is not allowed unless with written permission from the publisher. All rights reserved.

The information provided herein is stated to be truthful and consistent, in that any liability, in terms of inattention or otherwise, by any usage or abuse of any policies, processes, or directions contained within is the solitary and utter responsibility of the recipient reader. Under no circumstances will any legal responsibility or blame be held against the publisher for any reparation, damages, or monetary loss due to the information herein, either directly or indirectly.

Respective authors own all copyrights not held by the publisher.

The information herein is offered for informational purposes solely, and is universal as so. The presentation of the information is without contract or any type of guarantee assurance.

The trademarks that are used are without any consent, and the publication of the trademark is without permission or backing by the trademark owner. All trademarks and brands within this book are for clarifying purposes only and are the owned by the owners themselves, not affiliated with this document.

www.dropshippingpower.com

Table of Contents

DEDICATION	*12*
THE STORY	*13*
TIP NUMBER 1	*18*
TIP NUMBER 2	*19*
TIP NUMBER 3	*20*
TIP NUMBER 4	*21*
TIP NUMBER 5	*22*
TIP NUMBER 6	*23*
TIP NUMBER 7	*24*
TIP NUMBER 8	*25*

TIP NUMBER 9	*26*
TIP NUMBER 10	*27*
TIP NUMBER 11	*28*
TIP NUMBER 12	*29*
TIP NUMBER 13	*30*
TIP NUMBER 14	*31*
TIP NUMBER 15	*32*
TIP NUMBER 16	*33*
TIP NUMBER 17	*34*
TIP NUMBER 18	*35*
TIP NUMBER 19	*36*

- *TIP NUMBER 20* **37**
- *TIP NUMBER 21* **38**
- *TIP NUMBER 22* **39**
- *TIP NUMBER 23* **40**
- *TIP NUMBER 24* **41**
- *TIP NUMBER 25* **42**
- *TIP NUMBER 26* **43**
- *TIP NUMBER 27* **44**
- *TIP NUMBER 28* **45**
- *TIP NUMBER 29* **46**
- *TIP NUMBER 30* **47**

TIP NUMBER 31 — **48**

TIP NUMBER 32 — **49**

TIP NUMBER 33 — **50**

TIP NUMBER 34 — **51**

TIP NUMBER 35 — **52**

TIP NUMBER 36 — **53**

TIP NUMBER 37 — **54**

TIP NUMBER 38 — **55**

TIP NUMBER 39 — **56**

TIP NUMBER 40 — **57**

TIP NUMBER 41 — **58**

TIP NUMBER 42	**59**
TIP NUMBER 43	**60**
TIP NUMBER 44	**61**
TIP NUMBER 45	**62**
TIP NUMBER 46	**63**
TIP NUMBER 47	**64**
TIP NUMBER 48	**65**
TIP NUMBER 49	**66**
TIP NUMBER 50	**67**
TIP NUMBER 51	**68**
TIP NUMBER 52	**69**

TIP NUMBER 53	**70**
TIP NUMBER 54	**71**
TIP NUMBER 55	**72**
TIP NUMBER 56	**73**
TIP NUMBER 57	**74**
TIP NUMBER 58	**75**
TIP NUMBER 59	**76**
TIP NUMBER 60	**77**
TIP NUMBER 61	**78**
TIP NUMBER 62	**79**
TIP NUMBER 63	**80**

TIP NUMBER 64   81

TIP NUMBER 65   82

TIP NUMBER 66   83

TIP NUMBER 67   84

TIP NUMBER 68   85

TIP NUMBER 69   86

TIP NUMBER 70   87

TIP NUMBER 71   88

TIP NUMBER 72   89

TIP NUMBER 73   90

TIP NUMBER 74   91

TIP NUMBER 75	**92**
TIP NUMBER 76	**93**
TIP NUMBER 77	**94**
TIP NUMBER 78	**96**
TIP NUMBER 79	**97**
TIP NUMBER 80	**98**
TIP NUMBER 81	**100**
TIP NUMBER 82	**101**
TIP NUMBER 83	**103**
TIP NUMBER 84	**104**
TIP NUMBER 85	**105**

TIP NUMBER 86   **_106_**

TIP NUMBER 87   **_107_**

TIP NUMBER 88   **_108_**

Dedication

I wanted to say a big thank you to my extended team who is working with me on the eBay business. They have helped and are still helping to go ahead, work against all the challenges we are facing with eBay and PayPal.

Special thanks to my team members Maria, Robert, Jason, Morris. Friends and coaches Andris, Audrius, Edita, Romualdas and George.
My special thanks are to my support team: my smart, beautiful and loving wife **Ieva** and my little miracle - daughter **Upé**. Without you guys, neither this list nor business would have NEVER appeared on this planet.

Thank you,

Tomas

The Story

Hey,

Thanks for purchasing my first book. I wrote it especially for you. I know that you are the one who is seeking knowledge "how to?" succeed in business or especially in eBay business.

Either you are drop-shipping or selling your own inventory this book will suit you very well. I was doing both business models.

Before we dive into the tips and tricks section I must tell you about myself.

I am Tomas and I am an entrepreneur from Lithuania. One day I was wondering about myself and thinking about my past. It was the day when I was trying to understand why I like to build my own path to success and why I hate or cannot stand the corporate infrastructure?

I did a few major tests to understand myself.

What is my personality?

What strengths and weaknesses do I have?

How can I empower and utilise my strength and weaknesses 100%?

I highly suggest you doing 16 personalities **[16personalities.com]** and Tony Robbins Research **DISC** tests. These tests are free of charge so you can compare them and discover new facts about yourself. I am not affiliated with these companies, this is just a suggestion to start understanding more about yourself.

I think self-analysis is very important to see where you can adapt yourself in this fast-changing world. Knowing and discovering your full potential you can become unstoppable even if you need to build extra skills and knowledge.

So, when and where it has all started?

One day I was thinking about my past especially when I was around 8-11 years old. This was the period of my life when I was involved in my first business venture.

It happened in summer of 1992. One day my parents decided to go to my grandmother's allotment outside Kaunas. We had a small piece of land with an unused garden full of plums and other berries. Garden had eighteen massive plum trees around 5-7 meters height. These trees had thousands and thousands of yellow plums everywhere. Like little golden nuggets they were shining everywhere between small green leaves.

Suddenly, my dad told me that I could pick them up and sell in the local marketplace. All the money which I would earn from sales, I would be able to keep as a reward for my hard work.

All those little golden nuggets were encouraging me to do some work and exchange them to real money. I was very excited.

Within five days of my trading, I sold all my plums - around 100 litres or ten buckets. I earned seven hundred and thirty "vagnorka". Vagnorka was a temporary currency in Lithuania after gained independence in 1990. That summer Litas our official currency took the reign over Vagnorka. After exchange for official currency, my earnings were seven Litas and thirty cents. Yes, the ratio was 1 litas to 100 vagnorka. Still, I was a very happy kid making my first money.

This short story inspires me even today that we have so many different ways to earn money. We tend to think that this way of making money is not for us and we start searching for harder ones. Yes, you might say it is a seasonal sale, but all farmers are adapted to these patterns, the same as eBay sellers.

My venture finished that year and I did not have any other opportunity to do so, because my grandmother sold the allotment to somebody else. However, it was a great opportunity at this age to learn what customer service was, how to sell more, how to adjust prices and probably find the unique selling point to sell plums with higher profits than competitors. You will raise a question what is USP - I would say that when you are a kid, you are a unique selling point. I think people feel more empathy to the kids at the market rather than to a grumpy old guy or a lady who are already tired of the day to day routine in the farms.

Ten years later I finished Santara Gymnasium and got my place at the Kaunas University of Technology. I got into applied physics.

At school, I loved physics, mathematics and chemistry, but when I entered university everything changed. Actually, I wanted to study music and fulfil my dream, but the music department required musical education which I did not have at that moment. A couple years later I moved to Northern Ireland where I became a plastic bottles packer at Primepac Ltd. Within months I became a forklift driver and later on a sales admin. I can tell you I loved that place, but I was striving to fulfil my dream in the music industry.

A couple of years later I moved to London. Worked in a couple of places and was creating electronic music. Accidentally my track was signed by a record label Stripped Recordings and finally, I released my first single. I was over the moon.

Following this inspiration, I decided to hire a few guys to make a video clip for my track. Back in my childhood, I was always wondering how Madonna or any other top artists ended up on **MTV**. But as they say, when you trust the Universe you will end up where you supposed to be. Yes, MTV signed my video clip. 2008 was pretty much enormous year. Apart of MTV, I got a place at **London South Bank University**. Studied BA Music and Sonic Media. I really loved the course and three years past by so quickly that I couldn't understand where that time disappeared.

In 2011 I realised that I ticked my music passion box and decided to build something bigger. I had balls to compete with big boys in electronic music by launching my own music store. Big boys, I mean like Beatport, iTunes, JunoDownload and similar to those ones. I had a massive growth during a few years before we had to shut our project down due to Spotify's streaming service overruling the industry.

However, in 2016 I started searching for a new path to build my new business. I found a few people who started advertising their courses about FBA and dropshipping. I thought that dropshipping was the right business to start that requires a really small investment.

Here I am with the full list of tips and tricks which made my eBay store to shoot up to 200% in sales per month. I can allow myself to brag that even eBay Concierge Service specialists were asking how I was able to reach my numbers! My only one answer was: we are a strong team and working hard towards our goals!

Good luck applying all these tips and make your business happen!

Subscribe *dropshippingpower.com* Newsletter!

Stay on Top Of The Game!

Tip Number 1

I find this tip beneficial for those who need funds as it will save you a lot of money for sure. Especially, if you are selling lots of items. Lots of eBay users do not notice that they have used up their free 20 listings. To avoid paying the listing insertion fee, all you need to do is look out for the free listing days. eBay normally highlight how many free listings you have during the next 30-day period. This information is displayed in the Seller's Hub > Promotional Offers section. If you cannot see this information you need to customise your Seller's Hub, watch the tutorial here: **www.dropshippingpower.com**

Tip Number 2

Keywords, keywords, keywords! Keywords are the key for your listing to be found on eBay and Google platforms. Thereupon, thinking of a correct way to name your item means that it will be easier for everyone to look for it even if SEO is giving you troubles. Think about six or seven keywords which are VERY relevant to your product and build your listing's title. If you are facing challenges in strategising keywords do not forget to look at our website **www.dropshippingpower.com**

Tip Number 3

How to find the hottest items on the planet? I highly recommend digging into Alibaba, Amazon and AliExpress. These platforms highlight the top-selling items. Therefore, you can choose either the top-selling items to sell on your account or the similar ones. If your store is selling specific niches like electronics, toys etc., I highly recommend following the niches leaders and the information sources e.g. if you are selling electronics and devices check **Gizmodo**, **Mashable** and the **Youtube** influencers in the field.

Tip Number 4

To make great sales you need to describe what you are selling. Create a solid description for your item and use the authentic keywords' tactics. If you are making your own description, then use some tricks from copywriting. As an example, you can add your personal touch, it will make a unique search result. eBay and Google will make different approaches towards your authentic listing and show it in a higher search results position. Therefore, you have a better chance of sale conversion!

Tip Number 5

If you do not know what to enter in the title box, you have to get in touch with your buyers. Well, the solution is very simple. Either eBay or Google is able to unveil what people are typing in the search bar most frequently. When you start typing the first few letters in the search bar, it unveils the full word, after the first-word the search bar starts suggesting the available TOP searching phrases. These are called long tail keywords. Longtail keyword is between three to five words. It will be easier for you to get to the top of the search results, without SEO strategy. Do not forget that your title needs to have the important item's preferences such as colour, width, height, length or something else which cannot be missed.

Tip Number 6

Everybody loves to do their shopping in a shopping mall. We prefer checking and trying products before purchasing them. It is the most important decision-making process when you can judge an item's quality and suitability for your needs.

When you are purchasing online you do not have the real touch experience. Therefore, when you are presenting your selling item online make sure that your pictures can sell your product.

Use these type of images to convince the buyer to make a purchase:
1. close up images
2. material comparison
3. material pattern
4. durability
5. item in different colours if you have multiple listing
6. highlight hidden or special features in the product
7. display product how it looks in everyday use

Do not add extra badges on your pictures. The preferable background colour is in white.

Tip Number 7

This is a tactic that will surely help you sell your item when your dropshipping item is in the auction listing. Especially, if you are selling an expensive item. Sunday evenings are the time eBay is at its busiest as buyers would try to do the bidding at the last minute hoping that there will be no one to fight back. Be careful though when you are aiming at different countries, you will have a hard time as their time zone might not be in sync with yours.

Tip Number 8

One of the oldest trick in attracting customers is eye-catching images.

Yes, but what is eye-catching?

When I want to attract more sales to my store I choose one image which other sellers are not using i.e. product in the picture is shown from a different angle.

Change its background to yellow instead of white. Try to avoid badges like "fast delivery", "great service", "100% guaranteed" - eBay and Google Marketplace do not like this. The background must be clear and in one colour. Leave other pictures with a white background.

Check examples on our website: **www.dropshippingpower.com**

Tip Number 9

The correct category is the key to make more sales.

Preparing to list your first item on eBay marketplace make sure you know which category and sub-category suit your item. This is a challenge to all newbies who do not know how to do it and spend a lot of time just fishing around for correct category and sub-category.

The 3rd party listing tool selects the correct category for your item. If you think that the selected category and sub-category is incorrect, then you can select it manually.

Check more about categories and the great tool for listing your items: **www.dropshippingpower.com**

Tip Number 10

If you feel like there is something wrong with your listings, this can be due to a couple of reasons so be sure to use a hit counter. If you cannot do so, follow how many views you have got on your listings.

As per my experience, if the hits are low I would check the category, the description and the images. One of these definitely fails. Do not forget within 24 hours to do a search of your listing yourself. If you cannot find it, contact eBay for assistance or try to reload your listing.

eBay claims that the search result comes on the system immediately, but from our experience, we can see that a boost of views and an increased conversion starts after 48 hour period.

Do not stress yourself if the numbers are low for the first 48 hours.

Tip Number 11

Simplicity is the key. Yes, keep your listings very simple and attractive. If you need a special design, I highly recommend visiting our website www.dropshippingpower.com. We can create you bespoke listing templates. You will be able to have a simple and an effective template for your store.

Tip Number 12

We live in the 21st century and we can browse millions of professional web pages which are very attractive.

Clean and neat as the British say.

Maybe this is my taste, but the majority sellers and including drop shippers choose really unprofessional and messy, as I mention in previous tip, complex listing templates.

DO NOT DO THAT!

Some images are stretched through the whole listing in width or in length, distasteful colour pallet, funny images sometimes look simply revolting.

This looks like early 90's when the internet was released to the public and people who did not know how to program websites were creating them in a distasteful way.

P.S.

Avoid animation such as .gif files, video files are not allowed on eBay. Do not use links from Youtube and similar websites either.

Tip Number 13

When you are browsing your favourite website, you want a loading time to be as short as possible. Let's say within 3-5 seconds. It means that a website has optimised and compressed images.

Having this in mind, we now know that slow loading images make the buyer to leave your store and shop somewhere else.

Optimise your graphics with image editing software such as Pixelmator or Photoshop if you do not have any of these you can use image compressor online. Check our website for the link to the compressor **www.dropshippingpower.com**

Tip Number 14

Avoid describing something as "awesome" or "rare"!

Using this type of words usually indicates that you are an amateur seller. This just shows how limited your abilities are in describing what you are selling accurately.

Also, avoid these words in your title. It kills your title's 80 characters space. Customers do not search for items with these phrases.

Have you ever gone to the store and asked to show you a rare pen or an awesome toothbrush? Sellers do not describe their products in this way. Therefore, you will not find such words in the title.

Tip Number 15

Promote your listings and keep all your advantages to yourself. Yes, you will pay for advertising only when the conversion will be completed. But this will help you to escape grouped product pages. Buyers who click on the promoted links will be taken to your specific listings.

Cha-ching!

If you need a calculator to find out how much you will be paying for promotional listings visit our
website: **www.dropshippingpower.com**

Tip Number 16

As you see on many Facebook business pages, each of them has a little badge saying: "Responding Very Fast, "Responding within 24 hours", or "Responding time very slow". Which one are you?

Follow your "Responding Fast or Super Fast" strategy. Customers are always raising questions about your items. They think that there is missing information on your listings. 90% of these customers normally are on the verge to make a purchase after your response.

Answer their questions within minutes or a few hours, the same customer will place an order. Otherwise, they will ask you more questions. Be patient and help them to make the right decision.

Tip Number 17

If you just a starter seller or drop shipper obviously you will think how can you compete with others? How can you attract more customers? How can you convert more sales?

Always read what eBay is releasing in their news feed and contact them to discuss in depth about new updates. Ask how you can use those updates towards your advantage. eBay team is always happy to help you to grow your business.

You have got the edge on this if you are going to familiarize yourself as early as possible before the update kicks in.

Proactive sellers grow their stores within two months easily. You can have a store with up to ten thousand items and half a million either USD or GBP limits. According to eBay, this size store is BIG and you are a BIG SELLER.

Tip Number 18

Check each top-selling brands with its respective category. Do not forget eBay's VeRo program which does not allow to resell top brands (trademarked ones) and certain items' categories such as drugs, ammo, firearms, food and others. This is the best way to recognise what inventory you need to have in your store.
For more information check our
website **www.dropshippingpower.com**

Tip Number 19

Become a verified eBay member through their ID verification process.

Being verified is a big thing as it will get you past their restrictions. Also, if you are running your eBay account as a business, register your TAX ID, Business Registration ID and VAT. This will help you reach better results with eBay when you face challenges and need to find resolutions. The same rules apply to your PayPal account.

Tip Number 20

Choose your eBay ID wisely.

Having a name that is descriptive and identifiable with what you are selling is a big thing. Your store ID will help people search for you and your items easier. Do not copy other sellers' names. They can spot that and give you a hard time with eBay.

If you are selling technology items choose your name that relates to technology

TechnologyWarehouse

TechWarehouseUK or TechWarehouseUS

TeschnologyShop or TechShop

If you are selling goods for animals you can call it MyPetStore MyPetStoreUK or MyPetStoreUS – use your creativity.

Try to avoid crazy numbers combinations such as MyStore00258 or 15625ShopTillYouDrop

Tip Number 21

eBay is not keen on sellers using inappropriate language. This is not limited to listings. It includes posts on community pages, HTML and JavaScript functions, and on the external web pages that you link to eBay.

It is the best practice to avoid using any language that could be perceived as offensive.

Tip Number 22

Turn on the eBay RSS feed!

The eBay RSS feed allows eBay buyers, and subscribers to receive automatic product listings updates.

Turn the eBay RSS feed on in your marketing area. Then you will see RSS tag in your store's footer at the bottom of the screen.

RSS feed will drive traffic by distributing your fixed price listings, and even send updated prices for your customers.

Do not miss this opportunity!

Tip Number 23

Register your store domain name. Once you have established your custom store page and defined a home page then purchase a domain matching your brand name or eBay user ID. Next, redirect it to your eBay store's homepage.

A short web address allows your customers an easy and direct way to find your store and helps you start building Google search rank.

More than anything else, a simple redirect to our store increased our visibility on Google's product search. Once our items started being ranked on Google, we saw a significant growth in sales too. It also feels great to start establishing your own little brand on the internet through your domain name.

Tip Number 24

Email marketing will help you build brand awareness and will connect you to your current customers. It keeps them interested in your product offerings long after their first purchase and, if you aspire to build a brand beyond eBay, it is your best option to raise your profile. Open email marketing tab and press the "Create Email" button. It will display some pre-built email templates to get you going in the right direction. We use a combination of narrative marketing, just telling our customers what we are up to, with displaying current and new offerings. Readers are more inclined to check out your wares if you can humanize your brand a little, so do not be afraid to tell them your story and what updates are on the way.

Email marketing can boost your sales by 57%.

How to use email marketing on eBay check here: **www.dropshippingpower.com**

Tip Number 25

Now that you have started to build your store's followers make sure to reinforce your brand by including your domain on all your packing slips, package inserts, and follow-up emails. You can also try your hand at some custom stickers. For a few cents each, it can be an inexpensive way to help your brand stand out from "just another eBay seller".

Printed marketing inserts reinforce who you are and help your customers find you again when they are ready for another purchase. It also shows them that you are proud of your brand, online store and take your business seriously. Increasing buyers' confidence can reduce your return rate and make customer interactions easier next time, as you have already built some trust into the transactions.

If you are dropshipping and utilising Amazon.com or Amazon.co.uk Prime service, you can add a "thank you" slip. I am always adding a thank you note with our brand's domain name. So you can utilise the same strategy on these Prime items and gain better feedback on your store.

Tip Number 26

Spreading the word about your store can be as easy as just sharing your knowledge. The more you know about the products you sell, the more you can define yourself as an expert.

Dedicate some time of your work week to helping others get the most out of your products, and engaging with them where they gather. While you should not directly push for sales through these channels.

Be sure to include a link in your forum signature or the author bio, wherever it is possible. Google will reward your store with an SEO boost just by seeing your URL around the internet engaging with new content.

Check these three places where you can spread the word about your brand: **www.dropshippingpower.com**

Tip Number 27

Sign up to the eBay affiliate program.

You will earn commission after your customers click a special link to eBay and purchase your products or even another seller's items. That is an excellent way to reduce your final value fees or earn some extra passive income.

Through the eBay Partner Network, it is simple to get some product ads displayed on your blog and start earning commissions. We found that building a few affiliate sites, while we were planning our eBay Store, really set us up well to enter the market with our own branded store.

It gave us valuable experience at content marketing and directing traffic.

Check tutorial how to sign up eBay Partner's Network by visiting: **www.dropshippingpower.com**

Tip Number 28

Keep up on security matters.

You need to be more cautious and safe when it comes to your account. You need to set your account's security to a maximum level. Choose wisely a long and a difficult password and two-way verification.

I am mentioning this because you can include a little badge or a little information for your buyers that their DATA will be safe and you are complying with GDPR. Probably you received millions of emails regarding GDPR back in May 2018.

This is a great trick to ensure your customers' DATA protection.

Who trusts a company who cannot comply with that??? Would you buy from a fishy store or a seller?

Tip Number 29

eBay has a feature called Second Chance Offer. You can offer your product to the second-best bidder if their bid was high enough to you. This option you can use when the highest bidder decides not to pay for your item. Otherwise, you can use this option if you have more than one item in your inventory and the second highest bidder placed the bid high enough.

You will pay the Final Value Fee only on Second Chance Offers, so you do not incur any other listing fees when you offer this option.

<u>Do not forget to note that the person receiving the Second Chance Offer is under no obligation to accept it.</u>

Tip Number 30

7 Top Bookmarks which you have to save on your internet browser are:

1. All Categories Search page
2. Announcements and news
3. Discussion Boards
4. Leave Feedback
5. Rules and policies
6. End my listing
7. eBay Fees

Visit here to save links on your browser: **www.dropshippingpower.com**

Tip Number 31

In 2017 eBay rolled out an automatic system, which analyses your listings for the 3rd party links and email addresses hidden in HTML code. I highly suggest understanding "eBay links in the listing" policy. You are allowed to promote your retail store in your listings by posting your store's phone number and address.
You are not allowed to use eBay listings to direct customers to an online page that provides more than simple item information. eBay expects eBay sellers to sell on eBay, not to use eBay to sell items on another site where they do not have to pay eBay fees. Do not use eBay listings as the direct advertising tool or links to your non-eBay store.

If you made a few links directing outside eBay, do not worry so much. eBay will highlight a notification in tasks section where you will be directed to the list of listings which must be corrected.

Tip Number 32

One of the hardest parts of eBay business is when people keep their personal and eBay business income mixed in one bank account.

It is hard to track down your earnings from your eBay store. I highly recommend opening a brand-new bank account where you can see how the cash flow moves. Also, you will be more confident in planning your eBay business.

Tip Number 33

Do not be reckless when you are selling on eBay. Always calculate, calculate and one more time calculate how much exactly you are going to make from the specific item before listing it on eBay.

If you are drop-shipping or selling random stuff then its even harder, because different items in different categories will generate higher final selling fees. Stick to the fees formula and bang on one category.

The formula is available here: **www.dropshippingpower.com**

Tip Number 34

If you are selling your own inventory from your warehouse and shipping is organised by you then keep records of that. According to your shipping supplier, you can adjust your price.

Remember you can adjust your shipping cost higher on eBay or include in the price.

Those sellers who are drop shipping from Amazon - shipping is literally free when you pay 79 GBP or 99USD per annum. In this scenario, the cost of Prime account towards the number of sales makes this little investment ridiculously low.

Tip Number 35

When your items are sold, send invoices to your customers through eBay's invoicing system. Do not forget to include invoices in your packages. If you are drop shipping from Amazon, you need to include a "thank you" note only.

Companies on eBay are buying goods for business purposes. They might contact you via a message with a request to send them an invoice. Use the same invoice issuing method via eBay interface.

Watch a short tutorial on our website how to issue an invoice: **www.dropshippingpower.com**

Tip Number 36

Think outside the box.

Do not sell the same items over and over again.

Check what eBay is suggesting on their front page "what is hot at the moment". Otherwise turn the TV on and check what major channels are showing during advertising breaks. It will give you a great sense of which products are trending in the market right now.

Tip Number 37

Remove your emotions from your business. Prepare yourself for all eBay changes. eBay is doing hard work to improve everyone's business. Yes, some changes are too radical, too strict. Do not be emotional. Adapt to changes and flow with a flow.

So far eBay shook a big number of sellers in March and April 2018. Everyone was receiving a lower level of sales. EVERYONE! If any issues come up, call eBay. Do not hesitate, deal with them.

It is just a business.

Tip Number 38

Do not choose to sell what you like to buy, be open-minded and choose to sell what others would buy. If you do not have a pet, so you do not know what people are buying for pets.

The more you know what other people like buying, the better the chances will be generating sales. If you struggle to find out, just ask your friends what they are purchasing for themselves.

I highly recommend visiting your local stores and supermarkets. Check specific product section in the store and check what is happening online with you targeted niche products. Ask sales assistant what products are selling in their store. They will be helpful! Believe me!

Tip Number 39

Keep in mind, eBay is a real business. Majority of sellers and drop shippers treat eBay as a "sofa business". eBay business offers much wider opportunities than you think.

If you change your mindset and think that this is your business, you will start searching for solutions which can help you to improve it! This is not an easy task to do, but if you want to be profitable, you will treat it as a real business. Discipline is the key to make success in this business.

Tip Number 40

Check what eBay resolution policies are.

These policies may vary from region to region. If eBay rolls out new resolution policies' changes, it might change without any notice. I highly recommend checking it on a regular basis in your selling region.

Visit our page to know more what resolution policies are available: **www.dropshippingpower.com**

Tip Number 41

Do not test new drop-ship suppliers on your real customers. Do not risk this one out as you will not only risk your customers but also your whole business in the process. Just try with "dummy" orders for close friends and families. If everything goes out smoothly, then that is the right time to start working with the supplier.

Check the list of suppliers which you can use for your business: **www.dropshippingpower.com**

Tip Number 42

If you are an entrepreneur and love growing your business think in terms of how you can improve your listings. Make testing templates "A" and "B". Sellers use this strategy to see which one convert more sales. Do not settle on improved one. Create a new test "A" and "B" and find a new solution. More tests bring better sales results!

Tip Number 43

Spend one day per week to keep track of the competition. This step will help you see your flaws and improve your business. I highly recommend checking at least 200 listings and comparing them to yours. What do you have in your store and listings and what you do not? Check your competitors' stores descriptions, images and Impressum. Copy and adjust to your business.

Tip Number 44

eBay business requires having some money even to start with. Cashflow is the main problem that you will be facing along the way, so do not worry too much about taking out a small loan* to purchase inventory and maximising your revenues during difficult times.

*This is entirely up to you to make a decision to take a loan or not - please check your financial situation first and consult with a financial advisor or an accountant

Tip Number 45

Good habits and good discipline will make good results. Create goals that are attainable and sustainable. Create a schedule when you are processing orders and replying to messages during your day. When you are managing cases and complaints. Finally, when you are dealing with eBay representatives. This is a very important step for your business success!

Find your daily schedule routine template here: **www.dropshippingpower.com**

Tip Number 46

Comparing yourself with other sellers is a big NO! You are going to feel inferior whenever competitors outclass you. So instead of doing so just stay true to yourself and keep on doing what you are doing without thinking about other competitors. This kind of behaviour can come up by comparing yourself on Facebook to your friends who are having a better car or better holidays. Stick your head on the plan and rock and roll. Do not compare yourself with Tesco, Walmart or any other big seller on eBay. You can become a big seller within two or three months!

Tip Number 47

As Gary Vaynerchuk says – "feel passion, bro"!
Be passionate about what you are doing. All great and successful people say the same thing! Passion is an engine to build something special. Even people with the highest potential at eBay fail. So be passionate about what you are doing if you want to succeed!

Tip Number 48

Have you watched the movie "40-years old Virgin"? No?
I highly recommend it.

The main character's girlfriend is a mediator/mediatrix on eBay. She sells people's inventory for a small commission, that what she did with the main character's collectables too. Anyway, watch the movie to see the love story. It is the easiest way to build your store's inventory and you can establish your business without having to spend a dime.

Ask your friends and relatives what items they want to sell for a small commission.

Tip Number 49

Advertise your eBay store's brand on your email signature. Even if you just use for your external communication such as suppliers, friends, colleagues or family. Use a little link and your logo in the signature with text such as: "If you need products or services, please visit my Storefront at the www.storefront.company." Everyone likes to check signature links.

How to create your email signature watch here: **www.dropshippingpower.com**

Tip Number 50

Use Zik software. It helps you study the top-sellers' listings. Using Zik you can copy your competitors' inventory and increase your sales.

Obviously, you will need to cut some prices down. Make sure that your prices are profitable ones.

For more information about Zik and it features follow this link: **www.dropshippingpower.com**.

Tip Number 51

When you are collecting payments through PayPal, use Aweber PayPal integration as it can help you build your own database of the past clients. You can re-market and up sell your past clients with new listings/products in the future via email marketing campaigns.
Check tutorial on our page how to use aweber with PayPal: **www.dropshippingpower.com**

Tip Number 52

Drive the traffic from the outside sources to your eBay store listings. It will help to increase buyers' engagement rate. For this strategy use social media platforms, your email database and PPC campaigns. This will give listings more views and better chances to make sales. Also, it will help you push the listings up in the search results.

Use this strategy on newly listed items only. If you have items with no sales, end them. Re-list new ones and then drive targeted traffic to them. Make sure you drive targeted traffic only. eBay Cassini's results are often based on conversion and engagement [time on page] rather than high traffic with a high bounce rate. Drive targeted traffic to convert, not just to get views.

Tip Number 53

At the end of 2017, eBay issued a new request to make all listings mobile friendly. If your listings are not mobile friendly, then you need to adjust them with a special code provided by eBay on our website. Check the code here: www.dropshippingpower.com. Responsive eBay template will help you to build your brand, increase conversion rates and brand awareness online.

MAKE SURE THAT YOUR TEMPLATE IS CODED CORRECTLY
Mistakes in the template could affect your eBay rankings

You can buy mobile friendly eBay listing template on our website: **www.dropshippingpower.com**

Tip Number 54

If you sell expensive goods, use BuySAFE fraud insurance to your buyers. It cost a small fee to sign up, but BuySAFE has plenty of evidence that shows that using BuySAFE in your auctions will increase your bids and final values much more than the cost of their service. Check more information at our website **www.dropshippingpower.com**

Tip Number 55

If you sell electronics or cameras, you can make extra money by offering a warranty on your products through SquareTrade insurance. Check more information on our web page here **www.dropshippingpower.com**

Tip Number 56

The golden rule to make more money when your stock is going low.

Increase the price by double, sometimes demand goes over the roof. Last year we were selling AirWick Vipoo – Amazon was out of stock. Only a few Tesco had it in stock. We bought the product for 4 GBP per unit and were selling for 16.99GBP. I know this is crazy, but we were able to fulfil orders from our home. Pure profit 10.20GBP per item. It was a golden nugget.

Check the stock which starts selling massively and what is happening in the market to assess your position by increasing your price due to stock's shortage.

Tip Number 57

Make sure you are ready for the three golden seasons. Summer season literally starts from May 31 to August 31 and then we are moving into the season for Black Friday, Halloween, Thanksgiving and finally the third one Christmas+New Years. Yes, all these three seasons follow each other, but it is the time to make money.

Depending on the season and the demand for the specific products, raise the price accordingly as an example for air conditioners increase the price during the summer season or umbrellas during spring and autumn.

Tip Number 58

Using "Good til cancelled" listings (do not to be confused with "fixed priced 30" which lasts for 30-days only and never gets renewed).

This tip right here makes life easier for those with very large inventories. The key is that your listing will be posted on eBay for a fixed price for a period of 30-days and once it is sold, it will get renewed. Obviously, you have to have more than one in your warehouse, but advertise as "one" item left in stock.

If you are drop-shipping your items from Amazon, it is easier to keep the listing alive because the inventory is monitored by Amazon sellers. If you want to know how to track your dropshipping inventory check this link here: **www.dropshippingpower.com**.

Tip Number 59

Lower your item's starting price in order to draw more bids or sales in. This way you will create the item's sales history and a better ranking in the search results. After gaining sales momentum increase your price incrementally.

Using this technique the rest of your listings will start gaining better rankings. Calculate the risk before lowering the prices.

Tip Number 60

Regarding the niche products or products targeted to the certain groups of people is very challenging. There are different types of people, so it is safe to say that we all have different tastes. We need to focus on those who are into specific kind of items as these people are having a hard time looking for items because the ones they want are the ones we call "unusual". If you have a specific niche like collectables be very specific by targeting with the title and the description.

I highly recommend to offer an insurance policy from the previous tips, for this category of items.

Tip Number 61

Go GLOBAL to attract more bidders and buyers. Think of it this way, just because this item is "in" country does not mean it is in other countries. Widen your target audience. You'll gain more customers.

You need to apply for the Global Shipping Programme to go Global. 99.9% of sellers with good feedback rates and sales/purchase history are allowed to sign up. Sometimes it takes a couple of days before your account is in the Global market.

Tip Number 62

Go for 10-day auctions. The more listings are in the market, the more chance they have to get noticed. The first couple of days may be slow and you may want to remove them, but last days especially last few minutes before auction's finish, bidders will go mental. Sometimes you can gain 120-150% profits!

If you pay for a Basic Shop package, you have 50 auction's listings.

Check our page where the number of free listings for auction and sales is indicated: **www.dropshippingpower.com**

Tip Number 63

DO NOT BID ON YOUR LISTINGS! Too many people do this strategy not only on eBay but also on some other platforms. There are many bidders who force the real bidders to raise up their bid. This is known as "shill bidding".

If you create a great description and choose the appropriate pictures, the bidders will bid high prices.

Tip Number 64

We live in a world where we can imagine that all people are nice and honest but not in e-commerce. Do not let yourself be fooled by consumers. Many people try to use scam tactics to gain more from you or any other eBay seller. It is very easy for consumers to contact eBay and claim their money back plus to get your item for free. Make sure, that you have a tracking number to prove eBay, that your item was delivered by Royal Mail, UPS or any other company which can provide this vital information.

There are some issues with eBay and Amazon tracking numbers. eBay does not want to accept Amazon's tracking numbers. eBay says that Amazon is their competitor, but the majority of eBay's staff do not understand why Amazon Prime tracking numbers cannot be accepted as a proof of delivery. However, we have a tool which can help you prove to eBay Amazon's deliveries. Check it here **www.dropshippingpower.com**

Tip Number 65

Block dodgy buyers! PERIOD!

To do this mission you will need to click on "my eBay".
1. Under the accounts tab, proceed to site preferences.
2. Under the 'my account' tab you need to go to "selling preferences" section and choose "buyer requirements".
3. Click 'show' in order to find the 'block buyers'.
4. Then click "edit" and find the box with the title 'buyers with a negative feedback score', then submit it.
It will be really beneficial for you as a seller. You can block specific buyers too. But justify it though, as not all negative feedbacks are from these types of people.
  Do not worry that you ban those buyers, there are hundreds of millions of great buyers on eBay's database!

Tip Number 66

Be prepared for refunds. Be responsible enough to accept that not everything will go your way. Such as items that get damaged due to the lack of proper packaging from you or the third party sellers. One more thing, that can lead to a refund is that the item does not match the description.

Even if you are dropshipping you can have an issue with damaged products, then a refund or a replacement may be your options. Again this is not your biggest issue because you are just a mediator in the sale, but it will require extra effort to deal with the supplier to organise either a replacement or a refund. The biggest cost on these issues will be the amount of time you spend on these cases, and if the customer is not that happy, it may be a nerve-racking experience too!

Be prepared!

Tip Number 67

A complete manual or great packaging will make it more appealing to a buyer. So, make sure to take this into consideration. If you are selling items which require, for example, some specific cleaning instructions please pay extra attention to the description and provide instructions on how to look after that item.

Tip Number 68

List all your terms and conditions and pay full attention on this tip. If you want to avoid difficult situations with your buyers, make sure you make your Terms and Conditions as clean and precise as possible. If you want to get a template of terms and conditions, check our website here **www.dropshippingpower.com**.

Tip Number 69

There are a lot of items out there, that what many call collector's items. Such as playing cards, designer bags, art, shoes, etc. These items are going to sell high prices on eBay as a lot of people are competing to own them. One of my recommendations is to talk to your local art galleries. Sometimes you can sell their item for a great price and receive a great commission. Last year one of my friends asked me to sell his collectable piece of art – limited edition by Lhoutte. We were selling it for around 15000 GBP.

Tip Number 70

Create a multiple selection listing. This is an extra boost to your listing among other ones. If you are selling socks, use multiple sizes and colours.
eBay likes items described in details and with extra options. Do not bother to create separate listings, which will state the same description apart size or colour. This kind of listings will not be ranked as high as you think
Check how to make a listing with multiple choice option: **www.dropshippingpower.com**

Tip Number 71

Have the correct terms and conditions stating how long it will take you to process the order and ship it to your customer.

If you sell your inventory from your home, then try to make a notice on the listing, that orders made before 1 pm will be dispatched on the same day. It applies for drop shippers too. If you normally take 1 day to process your order it is fine too, do not forget to set this setting and mention it in your terms and conditions. If you do not know how to do this, visit this link www.dropshippingpower.com.

Remember "eBay delivery calculator" counts Monday to Friday as delivery days. Your courier may deliver also on Saturdays and Sundays as Amazon does which makes you deliver faster and leaves your customers happy.

To ensure great customer service, my team process all orders on the same day, even if they are placed after 1PM. They process all orders which come before 5PM. People receive their items quicker, and you get better feedback on delivery, which counts on your Seller's status.

Tip Number 72

Sell for a cause! Working hand-in-hand with a charity is a fantastic way to raise some brand awareness and help people in need. Yes, this is marketing. Yes, you will give a certain amount of money for your chosen charity, BUT you can put their logo on your listings to highlight that you are giving something back. It will spike your sales believe me! Do not go crazy with a percentage, I normally give between 5-10% of our revenue to the charity. Returns are much much higher! Utilise this great way to give something back to the ones who really need your help. Choose your favourite charity from all around the world or local ones, it is entirely up to you.

Check the video how you can help charities: **www.dropshippingpower.com**

Tip Number 73

Learn how to buy from government and police auctions. These auctions can be a great place to find bargains, however proceed with caution. Make sure you thoroughly inspect the item before you buy, especially tech items.
Check the link here which auctions you can attend to find bargain stuff - **www.dropshippingpower.com**

Tip Number 74

Increase your bids and sales by using a short opening paragraph that promises something, and then deliver on the promise. Describe your item, but also write about its benefits and/or how it is used. If you have personally used the product, describe your experience. People pay attention what experience you had using this specific item instead of guessing what benefit will it bring to them. Use short descriptive sentences and keep your paragraphs three or four lines. These days the minority of people love to read long stories.

Tip Number 75

Increase your sales by choosing a capital city or a big known city. If you are drop-shipping or selling your inventory in the UK, I highly recommend having the company's address in London.

If you are drop shipping from Amazon you will not know from which warehouse your item will be dispatched. Therefore, I suggest choosing London as a registered address.

A big chunk of items is based in Milton Keynes and London areas. People are more confident to buy from the company registered in London rather a little warehouse somewhere in Newry or a place which they have never heard of.

Same in US, we chose New York as our company's address. It gave a lot of boost towards our sales.

Apply this strategy and you will see increased sales. If you are having issues register your business in London, follow this link here www.dropshippingpower.com

Tip Number 76

eBay is using PayPal as they default payment method. After the conversation with one of the eBay's representative, we found out that eBay will be introducing a new payment method, however, it is still in a beta version. Majority of people believe that PayPal is still part of eBay company which is not true. Yes, PayPal has its own way to deal with sellers and buyers. If you are a small seller in the UK, you will have this rate per transaction:3.4% x item's value + transactional fee of 20 pence. If you want to reduce PayPal fees, you must increase your store's turnover.

Check PayPal fees here and how to reduce them automatically: **www.dropshippingpower.com**.

Tip Number 77

I know how happy you will be when your eBay sales graph will start growing. All your excitement will be reduced by the payment processing company PayPal. PayPal has around 20k GBP / 30k USD limit threshold. As soon as you start hitting it, you will receive a letter or a call.
What will happen next?
Well, they have a right to suspend your account and attained monies. You will not be able to withdraw your money!
To reduce the risk to be in this situation provide all the necessary information about your business and verify your PayPal account.

Firstly, they will ask you to provide your company's details. If you are registered as a business, then you have to provide your VAT or Tax ID information.

Secondly, they will ask you to provide receipts and invoices, which can ensure that you simply have your own inventory. If you are a drop shipper, they will perceive your business model from your receipts. Do not worry too much about that.

Thirdly, you will have an interview with one of the business development and fraud department representatives. Oh, does it sound scary?
I highly recommend you be ready to present a business plan.
What are your plans for business expansion?
What marketing plan do you have for a couple of years ahead?
Where are you targeting your eBay business to attract more customers?
How many people are working in your company right now?
How many will be working within 6-12 months?
Be honest and excited about your eBay business.

PayPal is happy to mark your account with positive notes. Unless you will not be able to convince them about your growing business success.
I bet you will receive a great support from that department to grow your business and make more money for both parties.

P.S.
    PayPal does not like a drop shipping business unless they can hear and see that you have a strategy behind.

Tip Number 78

Feedbacks Feedbacks Feedbacks The biggest truth about growing your eBay business is to have a big number of positive feedbacks.

Sometimes you receive feedback different from the one you have expected. The only one option is to contact eBay's customer service.

You can easily remove incorrect feedback from your account if you really put all efforts: delivered the item on time, had great communication etc.

During the conversation with eBay, they check what communication you had with the client and what item they had bought. So it is an easy task for them to make a decision to remove a negative or an incorrect feedback or not.

If the buyer used misleading words and phrases like: Do not trust, liar, scam, fraud, do not buy, did not receive (even the story was opposite), avoid, "not happy because I did not expect that" (if the full description is provided) eBay will remove these feedbacks automatically.

Swear and insulting vocabulary is not accepted on the eBay platform.

If the customer left a negative feedback by mistake and you are 100% sure, that it was a mistake, you can send a feedback revision request to your client.

I highly motivate you to contact the buyer first and ask if they are willing to review the feedback they have left on your account. If they accept that they have made a mistake by choosing the wrong feedback option, then you will send a feedback review request. Otherwise, contact eBay customer service representatives to remove the incorrect feedback.

Tip Number 79

Neutral feedback is a big no for my business. I think you should receive either positive or negative. When people start writing neutral feedbacks, they might write more negative feedbacks not neutral. I count that your business must receive 99.9% positive ones and 0.1% negative, neutral MUST balance on 0.0%.

Tip Number 80

Positive feedbacks. The majority of sellers start forgetting to work on their feedbacks, especially the ones who just have started their business. You have to earn tons of positive feedbacks to weight one negative.
If you have earned 10 positive feedbacks, and suddenly you get a negative feedback, it can ruin your selling account. Your search results will not come up as high as you expect.
There are three different strategies on how to generate positive feedbacks.

Strategy ONE
If you are a starter, buy cheap stuff for 0.99GBP or USD including free shipping to your door. Purchase your cheap items from different sellers, avoid the same seller. One seller can leave one feedback on your account every 7 days. So after 7 days you can purchase something cheap from them again and gain another positive feedback.

Strategy TWO
Do not forget to leave a note attached to your products, that you are more than welcome to hear your customers' feedback! I highly recommend promoting your domain name. It will be an easier way to navigate to your store and leave feedback.

Strategy THREE
NEVER EVER IGNORE THESE TWO STEP SYSTEM TO GAIN MORE FEEDBACKS
   Step One
   Follow up your feedbacks!

   Step TWO
   Follow up message you can use once!

So, if you missed that chance, I highly recommend going through your items, which were delivered quite a long time ago. You can check if your items have a feedback sign or not. If not, then compose them a direct reminding message, that their feedback is important to your business growth.

If you need to know more and see templates for these messages visit **www.dropshippingpower.com**

Tip Number 81

Since we joined eBay and started selling items on this platform fraud department was working very hard on all fraud purchases. Since eBay rolled in lots of new changes in March 2018, we saw a dip in fraudulent purchases. Fraudulent purchases will not be removed from the system because people will find a way to steal personal details and use it for purchases.

Normally you can start indicating fraud when you sell a rare or a very expensive item.

We had a Lego constructor, which was pretty rare and the sale price was much higher than competitors. It was raising a question mark why did a customer buy from us. The nearest highest competitor's price was 100 pounds cheaper.

What kind of precautions do you need to take before processing such as orders?

Match addresses on eBay and PayPal accounts. If addresses do not match contact eBay or PayPal.

Sometimes you can spot from eBay address line. They can change the name, address, but they might not be able to change the city, state or county. Then it is a fraud purchase. How can you send to London which is based in Northamptonshire?

Contact eBay and PayPal immediately!

Before indicating that this is a fraud, contact a buyer. For example, we set the rule to call the buyer, who is buying an item which price is higher than 200GBP. If the buyer asks you why you are contacting them, just tell them that this is a protection against the fraud. You want to ensure, that the item reaches the right buyer and their data is safe.

Who wants to lose 200 GBP or 300 USD. I have not seen any money growing on the trees yet.

Tip Number 82

Item was damaged during the transit!

Oh NO!
The tip how to smell the rat! We had one lady who sent us a message a couple of weeks later after receiving her freezer. She claimed that the freezer was damaged during the transit. We asked to send freezer's pictures in. Such items are wrapped in plastic and polyester shield. We were very confident that the item was not damaged prior to delivery. The obvious evidence was that we could indicate shoe shape marks on it. It looked that somebody was kicking deliberately to damage the item.

If you have a similar situation, call to eBay and ask to speak to the manager on duty.

They will log in to your account and assess situation what your customer is claiming. We were asked to collect the freezer by eBay. The story did not finish there.

We did the first collection and customer did not wrap the item as it was required by the delivery company. So literally we failed and lost money on collection (that is what we thought – eBay is helping in this situation by covering the collection fee).

eBay asked to do the second attempt. Client refused to wait for the collection company and dispatch the freezer back to the warehouse.

The customer started playing around and asking for money because she had to stay at home and wait for the collection company.

eBay does not accept this behaviour. We put all our efforts to collect and resolve the case. However, eBay took over this case, did a refund to us and dealt with the customer. What happened next we do not know.

As soon something weird is happening with your orders, ask to provide evidence and involve eBay immediately.

Tip Number 83

30-day return policy

It really depends what products you are selling. If your items are used, not brand new and you want to give the 14-day return/refund /exchange policy, it is really fine. If you are selling brand new items, then I highly suggest you choose the 30-day return policy. It is a very rare situation that people decide to return items after 14 days. Therefore, an extension to 30 days will minimise a chance to receive a claim for a refund, return or exchange. Some sellers provide even the 60-day return policy. If you are drop shipping, that is barely going to suit you because major retailers and e-commerce giant like Amazon offer the 30-day return policy.

Tip Number 84

30-days vs 180-days

So here we go! Your policy versus PayPal policy and how you can fight it.

As I mentioned before some sellers may extend their return/exchange policy to the max of 60 days, which you can do too. Rarely you can see, that somebody extends up to the 180 days return/refund/exchange policy. Dodgy buyers are trying to get their money back and keep your item.

eBay does not allow customers to open cases after 30 days period. Therefore, people go via PayPal to claim their money back from you.

When you are dealing with customers via PayPal's claim messaging service, you have to defend your position. Your policy is not PayPal's policy.

You are and were happy to provide all services within 30 days. After 30 days you are not responsible for any customers' claims. If PayPal is having an issue with the customers' claims, they must deal with it not you.

This is one of the reasons why eBay is ditching PayPal as a payment provider.

When PayPal will take your case to review, I highly recommend to call them and state the same things about your 30-days return/refund/exchange policy. Do not give up.

PayPal will be in your favour because you show, that you are willing to do great service within the 30-day period not outside.

Tip Number 85

Interesting enough this sort of strategy was mentioned by the top strategic marketing business speaker and Tony Robbins's colleague Chet Holmes. Sadly he passed away in 2012 but left a very interesting point about highlighting what you are really selling.

He suggested every single title you are building for marketing material, in this case, eBay listing title - each word must start with a capital letter.

People are more attentive to the words with capital letters. Therefore, you will see the majority eBay listings titles have capital letters. Most frequently - every word in a title begins with a capital letter.

Tip Number 86

Bundle up! When you have your warehouse full of stuff and some items stop selling, it grows a little nerve behind your back. Sometimes selling for no profit makes more hassle, instead, you may wish to give it away. It might work as a remedy and can boost your customers' satisfaction level through the roof. Maybe it is sort of a loss for you monetary, but you might make those customers to repeated ones. They might start following your store or sharing on social media platforms mentioning what a great your store is.

Also, you will free up some extra room in your warehouse.

Tip Number 87

As soon you start selling on eBay, you start gathering data about your customers. You do not need to worry about GDPR, which was released back in May 2018 by the European Union.

However, you have to keep all the data safe. To protect your customers' data you must create long passwords to enter your account. To increase account's security use symbols like "@ ! # $ %" and number combinations. Avoid your date of birth in any of your passwords. Hackers can use it as a reference point.

You take a full responsibility to protect your clients' data. I do not intend offering you in any way what kind of passwords you must create – just use the best possible way to protect customers' data.

Tip Number 88

Do not commit a crime! Do not make any threats or harassments to those who you do business with. Do not publish any personal information or any accusations about them online. Do not place or re-sell customers' data to the third parties without their consent.

I hope you enjoyed reading this book and found right steps how to work on eBay business and boost your sales. I am sure that if you follow these tips and tricks you will be successful in increasing your sales graph by <u>more</u> than 200%. Everything depends on you. If you have any questions, you are more than welcome to contact me via www.dropshippingpower.com website!

And finally, if you liked the book, I would like to ask you to do me a favor and leave a review for the book on Amazon and do not forget to share.
Sharing is Caring!

GOOD LUCK!

Notes

BOOST eBay Sales!

www.ingramcontent.com/pod-product-compliance
Lightning Source LLC
Chambersburg PA
CBHW031433210526
45464CB00005B/2180